The Lord's Prayer
A Re-translation and Interpretation

by
Njord Kane

The Lord's Prayer: A Re-translation and Interpretation
by Njord Kane

© 2017 by Njord Kane. All rights reserved.

No part of this book may be reproduced in any written, electronic, recording, or photocopying form without written permission of the author, Njord Kane, or the publisher, Spangenhelm Publishing. You must not circulate this book in any format.

Published on: December 1, 2017 by Spangenhelm Publishing

Interior Design and Cover by: Njord Kane

ISBN-13: 978-1-943066278

ISBN-10: 1943066272

1. Christian 2. New Testament 3. Gospel

First Edition.

10 9 8 7 6 5 4 3 2 1

Table of Contents

Preface..i
The Lord's Prayer.............................1
The Father..11
Holy Is The Name...........................15
The Coming Kingdom.....................29
The Bread...35
The Morrow.....................................41
The Day..49
Luke 11:3 Complete.........................53
The Sin..55
Theft of the Light.............................61
The First Chosen..............................69
The Tribulation................................73
The Lord's Prayer Complete............77
Sources...83

Preface

I am by no means a theologian, nor do I pretend to be one. I am just a simply man with simple questions. While I was seeking answers, I ran across this discrepancy when translating The Lord's Prayer directly from Koine Greek (Biblical Greek).

The Lord's Prayer as given to us by Jesus Christ.

Is there a difference in the translation and interpretation of the Lord's prayer from what was translated and given to us by the Council of Laodicea in the 4th Century (363 AD).

Let us translate it directly ourselves and find out.

The Lord's Prayer

We get 'The Lord's Prayer', also called 'Our Father' or 'Pater Noster', directly from the teaching of Jesus in the Testimonies of both Matthew and Luke.

The Lord's Prayer is one of the most well known and venerated prayers in all of Christianity.

In the Testimony of Matthew, Jesus taught the Lord's Prayer during the Sermon on the Mount. Described in the book of Luke, Jesus taught this prayer when one of His Disciples asked Him to teach them how to pray like John the Baptist taught his disciples.

The Prayer is essentially the same in both the books of Matthew and Luke, save the version in Matthew is slightly longer in 'petitions'. It is also the most preferred version of The Lord's Prayer to be recited and represented in Christian art.

There are several versions of The Lord's Prayer in English, the first being the Northumbrian translation in 650 AD. A translation was made again by the Church of England in 1662 AD.

These translations were generally made from the Latin translations of the Bible used by the Catholic Church.

Since these original translations, the English language translation of the Bible really hasn't changed all that much. This is obvious when reading a version of the Bible which seems to be half written in 'Old English'. One of these such versions is the King James Version of the Bible.

Here is the **King James Version** (KJV) of The Lord's Prayer from **Matthew 6:9-13**:

> Our Father which art in heaven,
> Hallowed be thy name. Thy kingdom come.
> Thy will be done in earth, as it is in heaven.
> Give us this day our daily bread.
> And forgive us our debts, as we forgive our debtors.
> And lead us not into temptation, but deliver us from evil:
> For thine is the kingdom, and the power, and the glory, for ever.

The King James Version of the Lord's Prayer from Matthew is the most commonly recognized version.

Here is The Lord's Prayer from the same Book of **Matthew 6:9-13**, but in the **International Standard Version** (ISV) of the Bible:

> Our Father in heaven,
> may your name be kept holy.
> May your kingdom come.
> May your will be done,
> on earth as it is in heaven.
> Give us today our daily bread,
> and forgive us our sins,
> as we have forgiven those who have sinned against us.
> And never bring us into temptation,
> but deliver us from the evil one.'

Already we can see significant differences in both the translation and interpretation from two different common English language versions of the Bible. The appear to have the same basic meaning, but there are significant differences.

The differences can also be seen in the different versions of The Lord's Prayer as given from the Testimony of Luke. Luke's Testimony tells The Lord's Prayer as was when one of the Disciples asked Jesus to teach them how to pray like John the Baptist taught his followers.

The version in the Testimony of Luke is a sightly shorter prayer than in Matthew, with fewer petitions, but essentially the exact same prayer.

Here is the **King James Version** (KJV) of The Lord's Prayer from the Testimony of **Luke 11:2-4:**

> Our Father which art in heaven, Hallowed be thy name.
> Thy kingdom come. Thy will be done, as in heaven, so in earth.
> Give us day by day our daily bread.
> And forgive us our sins; for we also forgive every one that is indebted to us.
> And lead us not into temptation; but deliver us from evil.

This prayer changes from Bible translation to Bible translation and language to language.

Here is the Lord's Prayer from **Luke 11:2-4** in the **International Standard Version** (ISV), which reads as:

> Father, hallowed be your name, your kingdom come.
> Give us each day our daily bread.
> Forgive us our sins, for we also forgive everyone who sins against us.
> And lead us not into temptation.

So which version is correct?

Who wrote them and in what language?

The book of Luke (also the 'Gospel of Luke' or 'Testimony of Luke') was most probably written at around 80–110 AD by the same pen as the writer of the Acts of the Apostles.

Church tradition contends that the author was none other than Luke the Evangelist, the companion of Paul. Nevertheless, some scholars disagree and argue that it may have been written by one of Luke's followers. Most agree that the Testimony of Luke itself was probably written about 44 to 74 years after the execution of Jesus in 36 AD.

Luke's Testimony was written just 10 to 30 years after the Destruction of the Second Jerusalem Temple.

This was a very significant period of time for the Jews. It was a time of great turmoil because they'd just lost their sense of nationality and their most Holy Temple had been reduced to ruins. The Jews were scattered from the very lands delivered to them personally by God.

This event is mourned annually as the Jewish fast of Tisha B'Av, which is usually in July or August. Tisha B'Av is an annual fast mourning the destruction of both the First Temple (Solomon's Temple) by the Babylonians and the Second Temple by the Romans in Jerusalem in 70 AD.

To the Hellenistic Jews of the time period, it was a sign of the end, especially after the Destruction of the Second Temple. The Disciples and Followers of

Christ also scattered.

In this time period of Roman occupied, Hellenistic influenced Judea, Aramaic was the common language used in the first century AD and also was the language used by Jesus and His Apostles.

Also present in the region, besides Latin used by the occupying Romans, was Koine Greek (also called Biblical Greek). Aramaic and Koine Greek were the 'common languages' used in the surrounding region during the time period of Jesus and the Apostles.

In the time period centuries before Jesus, during, and a few centuries afterwards, Koine Greek became the dominate 'common language' which was used from Egypt, through Judea, and up to the edges within Rome. This was the time period of the Great Library of Alexandria. The library made Alexandria, Egypt the hub of all learning; and the language most used and written in Alexandria, Egypt was Koine Greek.

The majority of literary products from the Second Temple period of Judaism during the time of Jesus were heavily influenced by the Hellenistic culture of that region and were most often written in Koine Greek.

This includes the Septuagint, which is a translation of the Hebrew Bible from Biblical Hebrew and Biblical Aramaic into Koiné Greek (specifically Jewish Koiné Greek).

After the Destruction of the Second Temple, when the Jews and Followers of Christ were scattered out of Judea, Koine Greek largely became the dominate language. Koine Greek was usually the most common language used wherever they went and Aramaic began to be used less and less.

Especially to avoid persecution.

This is why the original letters and Testaments of the Apostles, such as 'Luke, Matthew, Mark, and John' were written in Koine (Biblical) Greek.

These letters from the Apostles, as well as the traditional Hebrew texts of the 'Old Testament', were later compiled in single book called 'The Septuagint'. This is what is commonly known as the Greek Old Testament and it was written in Koine Greek.

The translations of the bible which we have today, regardless of which language, come from these original papyrus scrolls written in 'Biblical Greek'.

Here is an image of a 3rd-century AD Greek papyrus of the Gospel of Luke written in Koine (biblical) Greek:

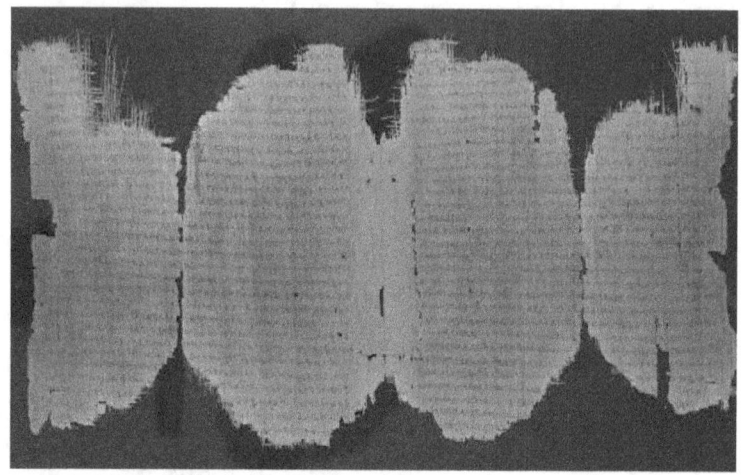

A 3rd-century AD Greek papyrus of the Gospel of Luke

Because these Testimonies by the Apostles were written in Koine Greek, this is the language from where we get our original translations.

There are none which were written in Aramaic, even though that was the language used by Jesus.

Of the Greek translations available today, the SBL Greek New Testament (SBLGNT) is the best resource available which is closest to the original Letters and Testimonials written by the Apostles.

It is also the Greek version most scrutinized and re-edited to match the original Koine writings.

Here is the **Greek** version from the SBLGNT of
Luke 11:2-4 *(ΚΑΤΑ ΛΟΥΚΑΝ 11:2-4)*:

Πάτερ, ἁγιασθήτω τὸ ὄνομά σου· ἐλθέτω ἡ
βασιλεία σου·
τὸν ἄρτον ἡμῶν τὸν ἐπιούσιον δίδου ἡμῖν τὸ
καθ᾽ ἡμέραν·
καὶ ἄφες ἡμῖν τὰς ἁμαρτίας ἡμῶν, καὶ γὰρ
αὐτοὶ ἀφίομεν παντὶ ὀφείλοντι ἡμῖν·
καὶ μὴ εἰσενέγκῃς ἡμᾶς εἰς πειρασμόν.

For comparison, here is the **Greek** *(SBLGNT)*
Matthew 6:9-13: *(ΚΑΤΑ ΜΑΤΘΑΙΟΝ 6:9-13)*:

Πάτερ ἡμῶν ὁ ἐν τοῖς οὐρανοῖς· ἁγιασθήτω τὸ
ὄνομά σου,
ἐλθέτω ἡ βασιλεία σου, γενηθήτω τὸ θέλημά
σου, ὡς ἐν οὐρανῷ καὶ ἐπὶ γῆς·
τὸν ἄρτον ἡμῶν τὸν ἐπιούσιον δὸς ἡμῖν
σήμερον·
καὶ ἄφες ἡμῖν τὰ ὀφειλήματα ἡμῶν, ὡς καὶ
ἡμεῖς ἀφήκαμεν τοῖς ὀφειλέταις ἡμῶν· καὶ μὴ
εἰσενέγκῃς ἡμᾶς εἰς πειρασμόν, ἀλλὰ ῥῦσαι
ἡμᾶς ἀπὸ τοῦ πονηροῦ.

Let us translate The Lord's Prayer, word for word, from its original Greek wording as given to us through the Book of Luke. From there, perhaps we can better understand its original meaning from the perspective of Hellenistic Greek and Aramaic speaking Jews during the time of Jesus into our modern understanding.

The Father

The first verse of The Lord's Prayer in the Gospel of **Luke 11:2**, in Greek, as was originally written, reads:

(Greek) **Πάτερ, ἁγιασθήτω τὸ ὄνομά σου, ἐλθέτω ἡ βασιλεία σου.**

And the first verse of The Lord's Prayer in the Gospel of **Matthew 6:9**, reads:

(Greek) **Πάτερ ἡμῶν ὁ ἐν τοῖς οὐρανοῖς· ἁγιασθήτω τὸ ὄνομά σου,**

Both Testimonies start The Lord's Prayer with the noun, **Πάτερ**. Let us translate that word:

Πάτερ (patér)

> *Father*
> Noun. (a father) "Father" in reference to a begetter, originator, progenitor – one in "intimate connection and relationship" *(Gesenius).*

Because this author of this verse was a devout follower of Judea-Christian faith, the title noun **'Father'** would refer specifically to: ὁ Θεός *(ὁ Theos)* the God, God the Father, God, Yehweh, YHWH, יהוה, the Father almighty, the God of Abraham, the Creator of heaven and earth, Father and creator of the universe, Father of all.

In general, the capitalized title *Πάτερ (patér)* **'Father'** signifies God's position of authority above the person addressing Him in prayer.

The title addressing Him in the prayer as 'Father' also recognizes His role as the life-giver, the authority, and powerful protector, often viewed as immense, omnipotent, omniscient, omnipresent with infinite power and charity that goes beyond human understanding.

However, the noun *Πάτερ (patér)* **'Father'** is without an article, such as 'the' (ὁ *(ó) masc*, ἡ *(ē) fem*, τό *(tó) neut*). This is because of its use in context and with it being capitalized, it is a proper noun but it is not His name. This is the context of 'Father' in Judea-Christian faith.

Throughout the Hebrew Bible (Old Testament), "Father" is generally used as a metaphor for God. It is not used as God's proper name but rather as one of His many titles of which Jews used when referring to or when speaking directly to God.

In Judea-Christian faith, addressing Him simply as 'Father' implies a more personal relationship as one would have with their own father. There is a deep sense in which Judea-Christians believe that they are made participants in the eternal relationship of Father and Son, through Jesus Christ.

Most commonly, Jews call themselves the Chosen Children of God. Christians call themselves the adopted children of God.

Both, as well as Muslims, also refer to themselves as the Created Children of God.

God being addressed directly as 'Father' is in part because of His active interest in human affairs. He acts and looks over humankind in the way that a father would take a personal interest in their own children. He is seen as universally being our Father, the creator, and we, His Creation, as being His children.

As a father would, He acts in accordance with what is in His children's best interests. Many believe they can communicate with God and come closer to him through prayer, which is a key element of achieving communion with God.

The noun Πάτερ *(patér)* **'Father'** used to begin The Lord's Prayer is addressing Him directly and personally.

Holy Is The Name

The rest of the verse of The Lord's Prayer in the Gospel of Luke 11:2 reads in Greek as:

(Greek) Πάτερ, ἁγιασθήτω τὸ ὄνομά σου, ἐλθέτω ἡ βασιλεία σου.

ἁγιασθήτω (agiasthētō)

sanctified
Verb. *aor pass imperat* of ἁγιαζω, meaning to sanctify, make holy, set apart as sacred to God, consecrate, purify.
Root words; prefix being 'αγίας' (agías) noun, genitive singular form of αγία (agía) meaning "saint"; and suffix being 'θήτω' used to imply the inner being, such as 'the soul'.
αγίας + θήτω = αγιασθήτω, directly translates as: Sacred Inner Being, Sacred Being, or Sacred-Soul.
Specifically something that is "Sanctified".
Most used as: *Blessed, Sacred, Hallowed.*

τὸ (to)

> *the*
> Article. ὁ (ho) m, ἡ f (hē), τό n (tó).
> (Epic, demonstrative) that.
> (Epic, third person personal pronoun) he, she, it, they.
> (relative, Epic, Ionic, poetic Attic) who, which, that.

ὄνομά (onoma)

> *name*
> Noun. Especially of the early Hebrews, a name was an inseparable part of the person to whom it belonged. In such that a person's name is also part of a person's very essence and sense of being. A name was much more than simply one's label. It is also their sense of identity and being. Therefore, in the case of the God, it is specially sacred".

σου (sou)

> *you*
> Pronoun. genitive singular of σύ (sú) second person singular personal or possessive pronoun: you (thou, thy, thine)

These four words, ἁγιασθήτω τὸ ὄνομά σου, directly translate word for word into English as:

"sanctified the name *you*"

The King James Version simply translates this as:

"hallowed be *thy* name"

The International Standard Version translates this as:

"hallowed be *your* name".

The last two words, ὄνομά σου (name you) is often translated into English as "**your name**" because English places the possessive second person pronoun (you) in front of the subject (name) and adds an r, changing it to "you**r**".

Second person pronouns are "you", "your", and "yours" and they take the place of a noun in order to address one or more persons.

In English, this is normally where the second person possessive would be moved in a sentence. In this case, the subject noun **Father** is being addressed with the second person pronoun.

Changing *name you (ὄνομά σου)* to *you name* and adding the possessive *-r (your)* is how most English versions of the Bible are written. The only difference are in examples such as in the King James Version which uses the Old English "thy" instead.

17

The use of "thy name", instead of "Your name". This is also a preferred way of biblical versing in English because the use of Old English makes the verse seem more sacred to many readers.

Normally the translation of ὄνομά σου as 'your name' or 'thy name' would be an acceptable, except there is an article before the word 'name' (*ὄνομά).* The word τὸ is written before the word 'name' (*ὄνομά)* and it is an article.

The verse in Luke is originally written as:

"ἁγιασθήτω **τὸ** ὄνομά σου"

which translates word for word in English as:

"Sanctified **the** name you"

or

"Blessed **the** name you".

If we take the original translation of the last part where we moved the possessive pronoun in **ὄνομά σου** from "name you" and changed it to "your name", we get how it is usually translated into Blessed your name. However there is an article unaccounted for when translating it that way into English.

What does the article "**τὸ** (the)" in the original writing of "*ἁγιασθήτω **τὸ** ὄνομά σου*" belong to?

Thinking in English, while leaving 'ὄνομά σου' intact as 'your name', if we insert the article 'the' and try moving the sentence around in possible variations, we get:

    Blessed **the** *your name*

    the blessed *your name*

    your name **the** blessed

It doesn't work in English, but we know that the article must be inserted into the sentence's meaning because of other verses and uses in the bible in comparison. In most English translations, the article τὸ (the) in this verse *(ἁγιασθήτω τὸ ὄνομά σου)* is usually changed into a form of being or existence by using the English word *be* or *is*.

But the Greeks already had their own words to express forms of being and/or existence. The Biblical Greek words ἦν or εἰμί are used as forms of being to mean '**is**' and '**was**' or even '**existed**'.

If the authors of Matthew and Luke meant the translation to be "Hallowed *be* thy name" or "hallowed *be* your name", as is in many translations, then they would have written it as:

    "ἁγιασθήτω ἦν ὄνομά σου"

Which would properly translate into English as:

    "Hallowed *be* your name"

But the authors of Matthew and Luke did not use the word ἦν they used τὸ, which is an article. An article they used in several other places in their Testaments. All of which were translated as articles (the) 1714 times in the New Testament alone.

If they meant it to be translated as **be**, they would have used the word ἦν or εἰμί as they have in several other places in the New Testament. An example would be the very first verse of John 1.

(Greek) Ἐν ἀρχῇ ἦν ὁ λόγος, καὶ ὁ λόγος ἦν πρὸς τὸν θεόν, καὶ θεὸς ἦν ὁ λόγος.

(NIV) In the beginning **was** the Word, and the Word **was** with God, and the Word **was** God.

These forms of **be** or **is** are commonly translated in English versions of the bible, but do not exist in the original writings of The Lord's Prayer. The original writing uses the article τὸ (the) directed at the word ὄνομά (name). We know this because the article is written just before the word ὄνομά and in Greek the article belongs to the word following it in almost all cases.

The Greek article τό (tó) is the neuter nominative and accusative singular of ὁ (the), unless it is used as a pronoun, then it becomes a pronoun.

With this understanding of the use of Greek articles, we can only conclude that something has to be missing or lost in translation somewhere with this verse.

In many religious traditions the name of God is considered too sacred to be simply written or even uttered. In Judaism, the pronunciation of the name of God has always been guarded with great care because of this. It is believed that in ancient times, the sages communicated the pronunciation only once every seven years. Because the name of God was too sacred, in every other case the name of God would be referred simply as: **The Name**

Which in Greek would translate as τὸ ὄνομά, which is exactly how it is written in The Lord's Prayer.

In Exodus 6:3, when Moses first spoke with God, God said, "I used to appear to Abraham, Isaac, and Jacob as El Shaddai, but I did not make myself known to them by my name YHWH."

The tetra-gram YHWH (יהוה) is the proper name of God as was given to Moses in the Old Testament. However, it's true pronunciation is lost to time. One reason for this is because neither vowels nor vowel points were used in ancient Hebrew writing. This contributed greatly to the loss of the original vocalization of the tetra-gram YHWH.

But the major reason for the actual pronunciation loss is because the name of God was sacred. The pronunciation has been intentionally kept secret by sages to prevent God's name from being used in vain. Besides keeping God's name holy and sacred, it also safeguarded from violating one of the core Ten Commandments, not to use His name in vain.

Some scholars suggest that the tetra-gram YHWH's true pronunciation is composed entirely of vowels, such as in the Greek spelling: Ιαουε. This Greek spelling is where we get the common English spelling and pronunciation of YHWH as Jehovah.

However this belief is put into question by the fact that vowels were only distinguished during that time period by their absence in use. This absence is due to the lack of explicit vowels in Ancient Hebrew script.

Often vowel substitutes were made in the pronunciation from semivowels and glottals known as tetra-grammaton. Even still, the tetra-grammaton was not permitted to be pronounced out loud, not even in prayer.

The proper pronunciation of the name of God (*tetra-gram YHWH*) is simply forbidden to be written or spoken. This prohibition on using the name of God is because of the commandment not to take the name of the Lord in vain.

As a Rule of Thumb to prevent from accidentally saying God's name in vain or to blasphemy, the practice is simply 'do not EVER say it'.

Instead of pronouncing YHWH, or any other variation of, during prayer many Jews will simply say "Adonai", which means "Lord".

Halakha *(Jewish Law based on the Talmud)* requires that secondary rules be placed around the primary law in order to reduce the chances of the main law being broken. Thus following Halakha, it is common practice of restricting the use of the word "Adonai" to prayer only as an added protection.

Alternatively many Jewish people, even when not speaking Hebrew, will refer to God by saying '**HaShem**' or 'haš·šêm' (השם). HaShem is Hebrew for "**The Name**". HaShem comes from two words: הַ (ha, "the") + שֵׁ (shem, "name"). HaShem (השם) appears in Leviticus 24:11.

> Leviticus 24:11 Hebrew OT *(from right to left)*
> וַיִּקֹּב בֶּן־הָאִשָּׁה הַיִּשְׂרְאֵלִית אֶת־**הַשֵּׁם**
> וַיְקַלֵּל וַיָּבִיאוּ אֹתוֹ אֶל־מֹשֶׁה וְשֵׁם אִמּוֹ
> שְׁלֹמִית בַּת־דִּבְרִי לְמַטֵּה־דָן׃

Leviticus 24:11 (NIV) The son of the Israelite woman blasphemed **the Name** with a curse; so they brought him to Moses. (His mother's name was Shelomith, the daughter of Dibri the Danite.)

Almost all Orthodox Jews avoid using either Yahweh or Jehovah altogether on the basis that the actual pronunciation of the tetragrammaton has been lost in antiquity. Many use the term HaShem as an indirect reference, or they simply use "God" or "The Lord" instead.

Another example of using 'HaShem' (The Name) would be in the Book of Psalms:

> Psalm 72:19
> בָּרוּךְ שֵׁם כְּבוֹד מַלְכוּתוֹ לְעוֹלָם וָעֶד (Hebrew OT)
> (Translation) Blessed be **the name** of His glorious kingdom for ever and ever
>
> (KJV) And blessed be **his glorious name** for ever: and let the whole earth be filled with his glory; Amen, and Amen.

Because of the Jews common practice of saying **HaShem** (The Name) and **Baruch HaShem** (Blessed 'The Name'), Jesus and the Apostles also being Jewish would have used these same phrases. Especially that of the later.

ברוך השם
Baruch HaShem
Blessed "The Name"

We can also conclude that *Baruch HaShem* would have been used by Jesus when teaching The Lord's Prayer to His Disciples.

The first verse of The Lord's Prayer in Jesus' language, based on adherence to Halakha, would have been:

אַבָּא ברוך השם
Abba, Baruch Hashem
Father, Blessed "The Name"

"Abba, Baruch Hashem" would have been translated in Koine Greek as Πάτερ, ἁγιασθήτω τὸ ὄνομά σου. The Hebrew word Abba ('Father') would have been translated into Greek as Πάτερ ('Father') and Baruch ('blessed') would have been translated into ἁγιασθήτω to express 'blessed'.

However, the Hebrew word 'HaShem' didn't have a Koine Greek counterpart in either words or expressions. The Greeks had always practiced naming their gods specifically. The best way to describe the meaning would have been **τὸ ὄνομά** ('The Name').

τὸ ὄνομά *(with the possessive pronoun σου (your))* is essentially the same thing as 'HaShem'.

Because Jesus was regarded as the Lord and the path to the Father, strict avoidance from using the God's name was not a custom in the Gentile world.

'The Name' became lost in translation in the Christian world where 'Lord' was the most universally preferred term to use. This is true in the

Islamic world as well where the term Allah is most preferred.

With this understanding of the Hebrew use of 'The Name' (HaShem), the first part of Luke 11:2 as would have been actually taught by Jesus, would be:

(Hebrew version) **אַבָּא ברוך השם**
(Transliteration) Abba, Baruch HaShem

Which in Greek was written as 'Πάτερ, ἁγιασθήτω τὸ ὄνομά σου'. In turn, the Greek was translated into English from 'Father, blessed the name you' into 'Father, most sacred is your name'.

(NIV) Father, hallowed be your name,

(KJV) Our Father which art in heaven, Hallowed be thy name,

The King James Version adds 'which art in heaven' (who is in Heaven), which personally seems unnecessary because most Jews, Christians, and Muslims believe that God is everywhere.

However, regardless of the preferred translation, the message behind this first part is clear and understood. The first word, Πάτερ (Pater) "Father", identifies and acknowledges God in a very personal manner as being the Creator and Father of all.

The next part hails the Father's name as being not only sacred, but as being too sacred to be uttered.

There is more to a name than just it being someone's label. It is part of an individual thinking self-aware being's sense of identity and being.

By saying 'Baruch HaShem' ('Blessed 'The Name"), His name is exalted as being the Most Sacred in all existence. Too sacred to say.

The Coming Kingdom

The rest of this verse references the coming of the Lord's Kingdom and it only has slight variations in translation which vary in length and stanza.

We know this part of the verse most commonly from the King James Version as:

> *Thy Kingdom Come.*

The original Greek writing is:

> **ἐλθέτω ἡ βασιλεία σου**

Word for word, we translate:

ἐλθέτω (elthetō)

> **to come**
> Verb. an act. "Come" used in the first case is the verb "to come" (ἐλθέτω [elthetō], a third-person imperative form, used impersonally, of ἔρχεσθαι [erchesthai], "to come").

ἡ (ē)

> *the*
> Article. ὁ (ho) m, ἡ f (hē), τό n (tó)
> (Epic, demonstrative) that
> (Epic, third person personal pronoun) he, she, it, they
> (relative, Epic, Ionic, poetic Attic) who, which, that

βασιλεία (basileia)

> *Kingdom*
> Noun. (basileíā) f (genitive βασιλείᾱς); first declension
> A kingdom, a dominion
> A hereditary monarchy
> The office of king
> (with passive meaning) being ruled by a king

σου (sou)

> *you*
> Pronoun. genitive singular of σύ (sú) second person singular personal or possessive pronoun: you (thou, thy, thine)

Translating from Greek ἐλθέτω ἡ βασιλεία σου

- (Direct English) *(to)* come the Kingdom you
- (Modern English) Your Kingdom comes.
- (NIV) your kingdom come

The King James Version uses Old English and adds to this verse:

- (KJV) Thy kingdom come. *Thy will be done, as in heaven, so in earth.*

This part of The Lord's Prayer refers to the coming of the Lord's eternal Kingdom as mentioned throughout the Bible.

> **Daniel 2:44** (NIV) In the time of those kings, the God of heaven will set up a kingdom that will never be destroyed, nor will it be left to another people. It will crush all those kingdoms and bring them to an end, but it will itself endure forever.
>
> **Daniel 7:27** (NIV) Then the sovereignty, power and greatness of all the kingdoms under heaven will be handed over to the holy people of the Most High. His kingdom will be an everlasting kingdom, and all rulers will worship and obey him.
>
> **Revelation 11:15** (NIV) The seventh angel sounded his trumpet, and there were loud voices in heaven, which said:"The kingdom of the world has become the kingdom of our Lord and of his Messiah, and he will reign for ever and ever."
>
> **Mark 1:15** (NIV) "The time has come," he said. "The kingdom of God has come near. Repent and believe the good news!"

This part of the verse / prayer acknowledges and gives praise to the Coming of His Kingdom.

The common translations into English for the entire first part of The Lord's Prayer in Luke 11:2 (and Matthew 6:9-10) fits well as:

> Father, Hallowed be thy name.
> Your Kingdom come.

With 'Hallowed be thy name' being an acceptable substitute for the Hebrew 'Baruch HaShem'. Especially with a better understanding of what is meant by "Hallowed be thy name'.

However the rest of The Lord's Prayer is quite different in translation from the original Greek. Different enough to warrant a deeper examination as in this writing.

Let us continue to the next verses and rest of the prayer. You will see the significant differences in translation which brings about an entirely different interpretation of the Lord's Prayer.

The Bread

The rest of The Lord's Prayer taught to us by Jesus is what gets my attention enough to examine the original translation and meaning so deeply. So let us on continue to the next verse, in both Luke 11:3 and Mathew 6:11, and you may understand why.

Luke 11:3 (Greek) τὸν ἄρτον ἡμῶν τὸν ἐπιούσιον δίδου ἡμῖν τὸ καθ' ἡμέραν
Matthew 6:11 (Greek) τὸν ἄρτον ἡμῶν τὸν ἐπιούσιον δὸς ἡμῖν σήμερον·

Luke 11:3 (NIV) Give us each day our daily bread.
Matthew 6:11 (NIV) Give us today our daily bread.

Luke 11:3 (KJV) Give us day by day our daily **bread.**
Matthew 6:11 (KJV) Give us this day our daily bread.

Already we can see a huge difference in the amount of words from the original Greek and that of the common English translations used in The Lord's Prayer in both Luke 11:3 and Matthew 6:11.

Let us translate this verse of The Lord's Prayer from Greek word for word as it was originally written in Luke 11:3

> τὸν ἄρτον ἡμῶν τὸν ἐπιούσιον δίδου ἡμῖν τὸ καθ' ἡμέραν

τὸν (ton)

> ***the***
> Article. (weak personal) him (3rd person masculine singular, accusative)
> m sg (definite) accusative masculine singular of ὁ (ho) m, ἡ f (hē), τό n (tó)
> (Epic, demonstrative) that
> (Epic, third person personal pronoun) he, she, it, they
> (relative, Epic, Ionic, poetic Attic) who, which, that

ἄρτον (arton)

> ***Bread** - not literally, but metaphorically as in "The Bread of Life".*
> ***Noun.***
> bread, food, fruit, loaf, meat, provisions, any food or substance. Also used in meaning the food of God. Used also metaphorically such as Jeremiah 11:19 *"the tree with its food"*, it's fruit.

In Hebrew .לֶחֶם (lechem) for food (for man or beast), especially bread, or grain for making it. The necessary substance for maintaining life. As Jesus was Hebrew, He would have used the term .לֶחֶם (lechem) which the Apostles wrote in Greek as τὸν ἄρτον.

In the second century, Origen of Alexandria explained that τὸν ἄρτον *(The Bread)* meant more than just regular food. He wrote, "the 'true bread' is that which nourishes the true humanity, the person created after the image of God".

St. Cyprian of Carthage during the third century referred to it as "the heavenly bread".

In the fourth century St. Jerome explained that *The Bread* is a super-substantial bread with greater meaning towards the future. He further wrote,

> "In the Gospel the term used by the Hebrews to denote super-substantial bread is maar. I found that it means 'for tomorrow,' so that the meaning is 'Give us this day our bread' for tomorrow, that is, the future. We can also understand super-substantial bread in another sense: bread that is above all substances and surpasses all creatures."

Tertullian in the third century wrote,

> "We should rather understand 'give us this day

> our daily bread' in a spiritual sense. For Christ is 'our bread,' because Christ is life, and the life is bread. "I am,' he said, 'the bread of life.' ...Then, because his body is considered to be in the bread, he said, 'This is my body.' When we ask for our daily bread, we are asking to live forever in Christ and to be inseparably united with his body".

The reference doesn't just mean "bread" of which we eat and get our body's daily nourishment. It is not a daily ration of bread which one would receive as a provision. This is not ordinary bread to satisfy one's immediate hunger and body's needs.

This is the divine provision, the 'Bread of Life. The gift of eternal life from the Tree of Life. "The Bread" is a metaphor referring to the metaphoric "Tree of Life". The essence of eternal life of which we were forbade in the Garden of Eden.

The Bread is a metaphor for the Tree of Life we were previously forbidden to eat.

This is the Bread of Life of which Christ offered through Him to reach The Father.

The Morrow

The verse begins with the 'The Bread' Continuing with the next part of the verse in The Lord's Prayer from Greek word for word as it was originally written in Luke 11:3

τὸν ἄρτον **ἡμῶν τὸν ἐπιούσιον** δίδου ἡμῖν τὸ καθ' ἡμέραν

ἡμῶν (émón)

> *our*
> Pronoun. genitive of ἡμεῖς (hēmeîs) (first person plural, personal pronoun) we, us, our

τὸν (ton)

> *the*
> Article. (weak personal) him (3rd person masculine singular, accusative)
> m sg(definite) accusative masculine singular of ὁ (ho) m, ἡ f (hē), τό n (tó)
> (Epic, demonstrative) that
> (Epic, third person personal pronoun) he, she, it, they
> (relative, Epic, Ionic, poetic Attic) who, which, that

ἐπιούσιον (epiousion)

> *for morrow*
> Noun. ἐπιούσιον is an unique word that isn't found elsewhere in the original Scriptures of the Bible, except in Matthew 6:11 and Luke 11:3.

By tradition, the most common used English translation for this word is 'daily' used as an adjective to accompany 'the Bread'. Most scholars today reject this because while epiousion (or ἐπιούσιος (epioúsios)) is often substituted by the word "daily," all of the other New Testament translations from the original Greek phrases into "daily" otherwise reference ἡμέρᾶν (hēmérān "day"), which would have also appeared in this verse if the author meant for it to mean 'day' or 'daily'.

The actual appearance of the word ἐπιούσιον (epiousios) in the Lord's Prayer of Luke can be viewed here in Hanna Papyrus 1 — "Mater Verbi" (Mother of the Word), known to scholars as P75, and the oldest surviving witness for certain New Testament passages — in the following image, 9th line:

Hanna Papyrus 1 (Mater Verbi) (P75), f. 1B2v
(Luke 11:1-13; the Lord's Prayer is found in lines 7-13)

Bruce M. Metzger writes in Bibliotheca Sacra 150 (July-September 1993) (pp 277–278):

> "The great majority of these hapax legomena occur also in other Greek sources, and so the meaning of most of them is not often in dispute. The meaning, however, of a word in the Lord's Prayer as recorded in Matthew 6:11 and Luke 11:3 has often been debated. Does "Give us this day our ἐπιούσιον bread" mean "daily bread" or "bread for tomorrow"? Except in subsequent quotations of the prayer, no other piece of Greek literature is known to contain this word. The only time it seems to have turned up was in 1889 when A. H. Sayce edited a fragmentary Greek papyrus containing a householder's account-book listing the purchase of provisions. Here, according to Sayce, in one of the broken lines of the list was ἐπιούσι—, with the end of the word defaced. It is most unfortunate, however, that scholars who wish to double-check this information are unable to do so, for the papyrus fragment has disappeared and cannot be found. Furthermore its loss is particularly distressing because Sayce (whose shortcomings as a decipherer of Greek papyri were generally recognized) may have misread the householder's list. And in any case, even if

Sayce did correctly read the word, lexicographers do not know much more about its meaning than was known before, namely, that the expression signifies either "daily bread" or "bread for tomorrow." In such cases when a word is susceptible of two equally legitimate renderings, translators have no choice except to place one in the text and the other in a footnote. —Bruce M. Metzger, "Persistent Problems Confronting Bible Translators"."

The Roman Catholic Church, the largest and oldest Christian Communion by far, instructs its faithful via the Catechism of the Catholic Church that there are several meanings to epiousios, and that "epi-ousios" is most literally translated as super-essential:

> ""Daily" (epiousios) occurs nowhere else in the New Testament. Taken in a temporal sense, this word is a pedagogical repetition of "this day," to confirm us in trust "without reservation." Taken in the qualitative sense, it signifies what is necessary for life, and more broadly every good thing sufficient for subsistence. Taken literally (epi-ousios: "super-essential"), it refers directly to the Bread of Life, the Body of Christ, the "medicine of immortality," without which we

have no life within us. Finally in this connection, its heavenly meaning is evident: "this day" is the Day of the Lord, the day of the feast of the kingdom, anticipated in the Eucharist that is already the foretaste of the kingdom to come. For this reason it is fitting for the Eucharistic liturgy to be celebrated each day."

This unique word, only used with the metaphoric 'Bread of Life', means "for morrow" meaning a "time to come" and not "daily" as is traditionally translated in most copies of the New Testament.

The Day

Continuing with the rest of the verse in The Lord's Prayer from Greek word for word as it was originally written in Luke 11:3

τὸν ἄρτον ἡμῶν τὸν ἐπιούσιον **δίδου ἡμῖν τὸ καθ' ἡμέραν**

δίδου (didou)

> *give*
> Verb. to give.

ἡμῶν (ēmôn)

> *us*
> Pronoun. genitive case plural of ἐγώ (egó); of (or from) us -- our (company), us, we.

τὸ (to)

> *that*
> Article. ὁ (ho) m, ἡ f (hē), τό (tó) n.
> (Epic, demonstrative) that
> (Epic, third person personal pronoun) he, she, it, they
> (relative, Epic, Ionic, poetic Attic) who, which, that

καθ' (kath')

> *for*
> Preposition. Apocopic form of κατά (katá) (used before a rough breathing).
> κὰτὰ́ (katá) (+ genitive) downwards, down from, into, against
> κὰτὰ́ (katá) (+ accusative) downwards, along, through, in, towards, during, for, for the, purpose of, according to, in conformity with

ἡμέραν (ēmeran)

> *The Day* (specifically **Judgment Day**)
> Noun. feminine of a derivative of ἧμαι hêmai (to sit) meaning tame, that is, gentle; day, that is, (literally) the time space between dawn and dark, or the whole 24 hours (but several days were usually reckoned by the Jews as inclusive of the parts of both extremes); figuratively a period (always defined more or less clearly by the context): - age, + always, (mid-) day (by day, [-ly]), + for ever, judgment, (day) time, while, years.
> a specific day coming, "Judgment Day"

"Give us that for Judgment Day"

Luke 11:3 Complete

Translating the verse from Luke 11:3, word for word, we have:

- (Greek) τὸν ἄρτον ἡμῶν τὸν ἐπιούσιον δίδου ἡμῖν τὸ καθ' ἡμέραν
- (Direct English) the bread our the morrow give us that for Day
- (Modern English) Give us the Bread of Eternity for the Day of Judgment
- (NIV) Give us each day our daily bread.
- (KLV) Give us day by day our daily bread.

From directly translating, in contrast to the 'standard translation', we already have a completely different interpretation of the meaning of this verse. It has changed from the standard 'Give us this day our daily bread' to 'Give the Bread of Life for Judgment Day'.

We went from asking for our daily meal to asking for the Gift of Eternal Life on Judgment Day.

And the next and final verse of the Lord's Prayer according to the Book of Luke.

The Sin

Luke 11:4 (Greek) καὶ ἄφες ἡμῖν τὰς ἁμαρτίας ἡμῶν, καὶ γὰρ αὐτοὶ ἀφίομεν παντὶ ὀφείλοντι ἡμῖν· καὶ μὴ εἰσενέγκῃς ἡμᾶς εἰς πειρασμόν.

Luke 11:4 (NIV) Forgive us our sins, for we also forgive everyone who sins against us. And lead us not into temptation."

Luke 11:4 (KLV) And forgive us our sins; for we also forgive every one that is indebted to us. And lead us not into temptation; but deliver us from evil.

Translating Luke 11:4 from Greek, word for word:

καὶ (kai)

> *and*
> Conjunction. and, even, also

ἄφες (aphes)

> *forgive*
> Verb. singular- ἀφίημι cancel, forgive; allow, tolerate; leave, forsake, let go, divorce.

ἡμῖν (émin)
> *us*
> Pronoun. dative of ἡμεῖς (ēmeîs) (first person plural, personal pronoun) we, for us, our

τὰς (tas)
> *the*
> Article. feminine accusative plural of ὁ (ho) of ὁ (ho) m, ἡ f (hē), τό n (tó)

ἁμαρτίας (amartias)
> *Sin*
> Noun. genitive singular form of αμαρτία (amartía). Sin, Transgression, Debauchery, Affair. Wrong doing.

ἡμῶν (émón)
> *our*
> Pronoun. genitive of ἡμεῖς (hēmeîs) (first person plural, personal pronoun) we, us, our

> καὶ ἄφες ἡμῖν τὰς ἁμαρτίας ἡμῶν
>
> and forgive us the sin our

Specifically important in this verse is the last part: τὰς ἁμαρτίας ἡμῶν, which translates as "the sin our".

In other words, τὰς ἁμαρτίας "The Transgression" is ἡμῶν "Ours".

This isn't 'our sins'(plural) in general, but The Sin that pissed God off in the first place. This is the transgression many call 'The Original Sin'. In the Book of Genesis when Adam and Eve ate from the forbidden Tree of Knowledge and were banished from Eden. When we fell from His Grace and were no longer seen favored in His eyes.

This action pissed God off and He's still mad about it.

On face value, what's the big deal? I mean, you put this tree out there in a garden and tell us we can eat from all of the trees, except these forbidden two. That's like having a big red button and saying, "don't push". We're going to push the button. Human curiosity simply overwhelms us. It doesn't take much to tempt us with anything really.

Well, we must understand the concept of metaphors and symbolism. The "fruit" or "apple" is not an actual fruit growing from a tree. It's a metaphor, say for example: the reward for your work. The Fruit of my labor. Th 'fruit' is what I have produced or made, here is the fruit of my labor. The result of my work and effort.

The "tree of knowledge' or "tree of knowledge between good and evil" is also a metaphor for ό λόγος (ό Lógos).

ὁ λόγος (ὁ Lógos) is the Greek word and concept for "Divine Knowledge, Reason and Logic".

What is the significance of this "Great Sin" of mankind stealing the forbidden "Divine Knowledge" (the Original Sin).

Theft of the Light

To understand what exactly the "Divine Knowledge" or "ὁ λόγος" and why it was a HUGE Sin to steal it, we must look to 'The Beginning' as told in the Book of John.

In the New International Version of the New Testament, John 1:1-5 reads as:

> 1 In the beginning was the Word, and the Word was with God, and the Word was God. 2 He was with God in the beginning.

Λόγος (lógos) Noun.

- That which is said: word, sentence, speech, story, debate, utterance.
- That which is thought: reason, consideration, computation, reckoning.
- An account, explanation, or narrative.
- Subject matter.
- (Christianity) The word or wisdom of God, identified with Jesus in the New Testament.

That's the basic definition of λόγος (lógos) and this is the part that gets my attention. Normally it is translated as "Word" and is interpreted as meaning the Word or Wisdom of God, identified with Jesus in the New Testament.

On a basic understanding I guess that is good enough, but there is a much deeper meaning behind the concept of λόγος (lógos) to the Ancient and Hellenistic Greek Period which influenced the author's choice in words in their writing.

The word λόγος (lógos) had a deeper meaning in Ancient Greece.

Lógos (Ancient Greek: λόγος, from λέγω lego "I say") is a term in western philosophy, psychology, rhetoric, and religion derived from a Greek word meaning "ground", "plea", "opinion", "expectation", "word", "speech", "account", "reason", "proportion", "discourse". It became a technical term in philosophy beginning with Heraclitus (c. 535–475 BCE), who used the term for a principle of order and knowledge.

Lógos is the logic behind an argument.

Lógos is what you use to persuade an audience using logical arguments and supportive evidence. Lógos is a persuasive technique often used in writing and rhetoric.

Ancient Greek philosophers used the term Lógos in different ways.

The sophists used the term to mean 'discourse' and Aristotle applied the term to refer to "reasoned discourse" or "the argument" in the field of rhetoric.

The Stoic philosophers identified the term with the divine animating principle pervading the Universe.

Under Hellenistic Judaism (the time of Jesus and the Apostles), Philo (c. 20 BCE – 50 CE) adopted the term into Jewish philosophy. The Gospel of John identifies the Lógos, through which all things are made, as divine (theos), and further identifies Jesus Christ as the incarnate Lógos.

Despite the conventional translation as "word", it is not used for a word in the grammatical sense; in the grammatical sense, the term lexis (λέξις) was used. So it is not "The Word" or "Word of God", otherwise the word lexis (λέξις) would have been used in John's Writing.

He used the word λόγος (lógos), which had a much deeper meaning than simply meaning God's Word. Had he simply meant 'God's Word', he would have used the word lexis (λέξις) and it would have been written as θεός λέξις (Theós Lexis). The author used the word λόγος (lógos) because it had a much deeper meaning which his fellow Hellenistic Judaism audience understood.

The concept of λόγος (lógos) in Hellenistic Judaism

Hellenistic Judaism was heavily influences by Ancient Greek thinking and philosophy. The concept o lógos would have been understood and discussed in great length by people in that day.

This must be considered when translating the writing of that area and time period.

The Septuagint (from the Latin septuaginta, "seventy") is a Koine Greek translation of a Hebraic textual tradition that included certain texts which were later included in the canonical Hebrew Bible and other related texts which were not. As the primary Greek translation of the Old Testament, it is also called the Greek Old Testament.

In the Septuagint the term lógos is used for the word of God in the creation of heaven in Psalm 33:6.

"By the word (lógos) of the LORD the heavens were made, their starry host by the breath of his mouth."
-Psalm 33:6 (NIV)

Philo of Alexandria (20 BCE – 50 CE) was a Hellenized Jew who used the term lógos to mean an intermediary divine being, or demiurge.

Philo of Alexandria

Philo followed the Platonic distinction between imperfect matter and perfect Form, and therefore intermediary beings were necessary to bridge the enormous gap between God and the material world. The Lógos was the highest of these intermediary beings, and was called by Philo "the first-born of God". Philo also wrote that "the Lógos of the living God is the bond of everything, holding all things together and binding all the parts, and prevents them from being dissolved and separated".

Plato's Theory of Forms was located within the Lógos, but the Lógos also acted on behalf of God in the physical world. In particular, the Angel of the Lord in the Hebrew Bible (Old Testament) was identified with the Lógos by Philo, who also said that the Lógos was God's instrument in the creation of the universe.

So, Lógos isn't the Word, but closer to the logic or reasoning of the living word. The conscious incarnate. Lógos is a being which exists as part of the self of God. It is the intellectual and conscious Will of God.

It is a being's very thought and will as a conscious essence. The free will of thought and action.

A being's very conscious and will. Their mind merged with the essence of their very being is what the λόγος (lógos) is in concept.

The λόγος (lógos) is the very essence of God, the Will of God, the very essence of reason.

This changes the meaning behind the very first verse in the Book of John extra substantially. It is more than a mere word or law or God. It is the very conscious being and will of God.

John 1: In the beginning of everything there existed the living essence of thought and reason behind free will,

So this is the Original Sin. The fruit from the Tree of Knowledge of Good and Evil. We stole the λόγος (lógos) which separated us from everything God had created and made us like us.

We weren't ready and He probably wasn't even sure if He was going to give it to us - so we stole it.

Yeah, he's still pissed about it. So pissed, he's going to toast the lot of us. He made that VERY clear - He's mad.

So Luke 11:4

τὰς - ἁμαρτίας - ἡμῶν
the - sin - our

Is the specific Sin of which He is talking about in The Lord's Prayer. The Sin which is Ours.

Forgive us for stealing the λόγος (lógos), the living will and essence of reason and logical thought. We stole the Light and became able to separate it from the Darkness (ignorance).

We stole Enlightenment. This was the grave Sin of Humanity. The theft of The Divine Light.

The First Chosen

And the rest: καὶ γὰρ αὐτοὶ ἀφίομεν παντὶ ὀφείλοντι ἡμῖν·

καὶ (kai)

> *and*
> Conjunction. and, even, also

γὰρ (gar)

> *for*
> Conjunction. for, since

αὐτοὶ (autoi)

> *those*
> Pronoun. Nominative masculine plural form of αυτός (aftós) these, they, them

ἀφίομεν (aphiomen)

> *forgive*
> Verb. pres act indic, 1 pl -ἀφιημι cancel, forgive; allow, tolerate; leave, forsake, let go, divorce.

Παντὶ (panti)

> *all*
> Adjective. all, as a whole.

ὀφείλοντι (opheilonti)

> *first-chosen*
> Noun. ὀφε is a prefix for 'first' often used in regard to the 'first' day of the week, etc.
> είλοντι is from εἵλοντο meaning 'to take, to select, choose, or prefer'.
> Είλοντι is plural of 'selected, taken, chosen, preferred', making its meaning: The Chosen, The Selected, The Preferred.
> ὀφε + είλοντι = ὀφείλοντι = 'the first selected' or 'the first chosen'.

ἡμῶν (émón)

> *our*
> Pronoun. genitive of ἡμεῖς (hēmeîs) (first person plural, personal pronoun) we, us, our

This part of the verse directly translates as:

> (**Greek**) καὶ γὰρ αὐτοὶ ἀφίομεν παντὶ ὀφείλοντι ἡμῖν
> (**Direct English**) and for those forgive all "first chosen' our
> (**Modern English**) And forgive the first chosen

This is asking for forgiveness of the "first chosen". The "first chosen" are the Jews who were brought out of Egypt and had made a Covenant with God.

The "chosen ones".

This part of the verse is asking for forgiven for Jews for breaking the Covenant and for rejecting Jesus as the Messiah. A rejection which led to His execution where He even prayed for God to forgive them by saying, "forgive them Father, for they know not what they do".

The Tribulation

The rest of the verse: καὶ μὴ εἰσενέγκῃς ἡμᾶς εἰς πειρασμόν.

καὶ (kai)
> *and*
> Conjunction. and, even, also

μὴ (mē)
> *not*
> Particle. not

εἰσενέγκῃς (eisenenkēs)
> *lead*
> Verb. lead in, carry in, bring in, deliver

ἡμᾶς (ēmâs)
> *us*
> Pronoun. accusative of ἡμεῖς (hēmeîs): us

εἰς (eis)

> *into*
> Preposition. into

πειρασμόν (peirasmon)

> *tribulation*
> Noun. second declension from πειράζω (peirázō, "to prove") + -μός (-mós).
> test, trial, proof, or tribulation

This part of the verse directly translates as:

> (**Greek**) καὶ μὴ εἰσενέγκῃς ἡμᾶς εἰς πειρασμόν
> (**Direct English**) and not deliver us to (the) tribulation
> (**Modern English**) and deliver us from the tribulation

This part is asking to be led or taken away from the "Great Trials" or "Tribulation". It is asking for mercy to be "Raptured" before the "Great Tribulation" and be spared from God's wrath and Judgment.

KATA ΛΟΥΚΑΝ 11:4
Luke 11:4 and forgive us the sin our, and for these forgive all "first chosen' our, and not lead us into trials.

The Lord's Prayer Complete

Translating Luke 11:4 word for word, we have:

(Greek) καὶ ἄφες ἡμῖν τὰς ἁμαρτίας ἡμῶν, καὶ γὰρ αὐτοὶ ἀφίομεν παντὶ ὀφείλοντι ἡμῖν, καὶ μὴ εἰσενέγκῃς ἡμᾶς εἰς πειρασμόν.

(Direct English) and forgive us the sin our, and for those forgive all "first chosen' our, and not lead us to (the) tribulation

(Modern English) Forgive us for Our Sin, and forgive the first chosen, and gather us away from tribulation

(NIV) Forgive us our sins, for we also forgive everyone who sins against us. And lead us not into temptation.

(KLV) And forgive us our sins; for we also forgive every one that is indebted to us. And lead us not into temptation; but deliver us from evil.

Let's put it the entire prayer from Luke 11:2-4

together now that we've translated it. Directly translated and then paraphrasing to match Modern English used today, we get:

> Father, praise to your sacred name,
> your Kingdom is coming.
> Give us the gift of eternal life.
> and forgive us for Our Sin,
> and forgive the first chosen,
> and gather us away from tribulation

Here is the King James Version (KJV) of The Lord's Prayer from Luke 11:2-4:

> Our Father which art in heaven,
> Hallowed be thy name.
> Thy kingdom come.
> Thy will be done, as in heaven, so in earth.
> Give us day by day our daily bread.
> And forgive us our sins; for we also forgive every one that is indebted to us.
> And lead us not into temptation;
> but deliver us from evil.

The Lord's Prayer from Luke 11:2-4 in the International Standard Version (ISV) reads as:

> 'Father, hallowed be your name,
> your kingdom come.
> Give us each day our daily bread.
> Forgive us our sins, for we also forgive everyone who sins against us.
> And lead us not into temptation."

The Original Greek of Luke 11:2-4 (ΚΑΤΑ ΛΟΥΚΑΝ 11:2-4) reads as:

Πάτερ, ἁγιασθήτω τὸ ὄνομά σου·
ἐλθέτω ἡ βασιλεία σου·
τὸν ἄρτον ἡμῶν τὸν ἐπιούσιον δίδου ἡμῖν τὸ καθ᾽ ἡμέραν·
καὶ ἄφες ἡμῖν τὰς ἁμαρτίας ἡμῶν,
καὶ γὰρ αὐτοὶ ἀφίομεν παντὶ ὀφείλοντι ἡμῖν·
καὶ μὴ εἰσενέγκῃς ἡμᾶς εἰς πειρασμόν.

I would dare take the Modern English version if it were delivered by the Gospel of Luke today, instead of being nearly lost in translation over the past 2000 years, as:

Father, praise to your sacred name, your Kingdom is coming.
Give us the gift of eternal life.
Forgive us for Our Sin, and forgive the first chosen, and gather us away from tribulation

and take it a step further by writing it as:

Our Most Sacred and Blessed Father,
your Kingdom is coming.
Forgive us for Our Transgression and forgive those of the first chosen.
and grant us mercy away from Tribulation and give us the gift of eternal life.

I believe this is the 'what about', 'how', and 'why' Jesus was trying to teach us when we pray to The

Father. It is not a prayer for bread given to us on a daily basis. He already gave us our daily bread when he created everything - the fruits, grains, etc.. for us to rule over. So why would Jesus tell us to pray for something the Father has already provided? Why should we pray for our deplorable daily sins and transgressions. That just hints "that's okay if you say 'sorry'" - To the Father, it is NOT. He's made it very clear on a number of occasions.

Jesus was trying to teach us to pray for what we don't have or what was denied of us due to our ancient transgression, such as the gift of eternal life. Something Jesus constantly reminded us about by using the metaphor of "Bread of Life".

He also told us to pray for forgiveness, not for small daily sins or sins made against us, but for the BIG grave Sin when we stole The Enlightenment from the 'Tree of Knowledge between Good and Evil'. We were not only disobedient, but arrogant by thinking if we stole the λόγος that we would be like The Father. We tried to be like God ourselves.

It is asking for forgiveness for stealing Enlightenment and humbling ourselves by recognizing that we are NOT gods by praising His Name.

It is asking forgiveness for the First Chosen, the Hebrews gathered by Moses who had broken His

Covenant with them. Not just that, but also for Him (Jesus) as the Messiah and having Him executed.

The prayer is about praising the Father and His coming Kingdom and asking to for mercy to be spared the Great Tribulation to be suffered before Judgment. To be forgiven and spared Final Judgment and be given Eternal Life.

I believe, if this prayer and message were delivered today, it would read:

> Father, sacred is your name
> and blessed is the coming of your Kingdom.
> Forgive us for our transgression
> and forgive those of the first chosen.
> and grant us mercy away from tribulation
> and give us the gift of eternal life.

Sources

- Francesco Di Geronimo Jovino. Disquisitio Critico-Biblica De Tempore Sepulturae Christi (Latin Edition). Nabo Press, 2010. ISBN: 978-1145433700
- Koine Greek of Luke 11:2-4
- Luke 11:2-4 International Standard Version,
- William D. Mounce. Basics of Biblical Greek Grammar. Zondervan; 3rd ed. edition, 2009. ISBN 978-0310287681
- Kata Biblon, Wiki Lexicon of the Greek New Testament
- James Strong. The New Strong's Expanded Exhaustive Concordance of the Bible. Thomas Nelson; Expanded edition, 2010. ISBN 978-1418541682
- Society of Biblical Literature and Logos Bible Software. The Greek New Testament: SBL Print Edition,
- Society of Biblical Literature and Logos Bible Software. The Greek New Testament: SBL Digital Edition
- Bible Gateway
- Bible Hub
- Aramaic Bible in Plain English
- Young's Literal Translation
- Mounce Reverse-Interlinear New Testament (MOUNCE)

- New International Version
- Henry George Liddell and Robert Scott, An Intermediate Greek–English Lexicon: logos, 1889. ISBN 978-0282484729
- Cambridge Dictionary of Philosophy (3rd ed): Cambridge University Press, 1999. ISBN 978-1107643796
- Frederick Copleston, A History of Philosophy, Volume 1, Continuum, 2003. ISBN 978-0385468435
- Philo, De Profugis, cited in Gerald Friedlander, Hellenism and Christianity, P. Vallentine, 1912. ISBN 978-1110357093
- Gibson, Jeffrey B. The Disciples' Prayer: The Prayer Jesus Taught in Its Historical Setting. Fortress Press, 2015. ISBN 978-1451490251
- Robert Leighton (Abp. of Glasgow). Expositions on the creed, the Lord's prayer, and the Ten commandments. Palala Press, 2016. ISBN 978-1357615680
- Commentaries on Matthew 1.6.11
- On Prayer
- King James Version (KJV) of The Lord's Prayer from Luke 11:2-4
- Luke 11:2-4 in the International Standard Version (ISV)
- Bruce Metzger. Persistent Problems Confronting Bible Translators. Bibliotheca Sacra 150 (July-September 1993). 223-84.
- Hanna Papyrus 1 (Mater Verbi) (P75), f. 1B2v

- Holmes, Michael W.. The Greek New Testament: SBL Edition. (SBLGNT) Society of Biblical Literature, 2010. ISBN 1-58983-535-2

- Alon Goshen-Gottstein. "God the Father in

Rabbinic Judaism and Christianity: Transformed Background or Common Ground?" The Elijah Interfaith Institute, Journal of Ecumenical Studies, 38:4, Spring 2001.

- James Orr. The International standard Bible encyclopedia - Scholar's Choice Edition. 1885.

- Edward Robinson. "Gesenius denies that elohim ever means angels; and he refers in this denial particularly to Ps. 8: 5, and Ps. 97: 7; but he observes, that the term is so translated in the ancient versions." The Biblical Repositor p. 360 ed, 1838.

- Samuel Davidsohn An Introduction to the New Testament 3 1848.

www.ingramcontent.com/pod-product-compliance
Lightning Source LLC
Chambersburg PA
CBHW050507120526
44588CB00044B/1663